MELODIOUS and PROGRESSIVE STUDIES, Book 1

FOR SAXOPHONE

selected and edited by

David Hite

Includes

Demnitz: 36 Expressive Studies

Nocentini: 9 Melodic Studies

Baermann: 14 Melodic Etudes

Kayser: 5 Progressive Studies

B-379

Southern
MUSIC

CONTENTS

COMMENT

The studies chosen for this volume have been carefully selected based on two criteria: First, the music is taken from proven, quality sources that are both attractive and ideal for students. Second, the materials are of medium technical difficulty. All the composers were artist performers and teachers who lived in the nineteenth century: Friedrich Demnitz (1845- 1890, Dresden, Germany), Domenico Nocentini (1948-1890, Florence, Italy), Carl Baermann (1810-1885, Munich, Germany), and Heinrich Kayser (1815-1888, Hamburg, Germany).

The progressing saxophonist has here an ideal musical challenge, allowing for concentration on tonal development. Tonal inflection for rhythmic emphasis as well as for melodic line can be stressed. The Kayser studies, No.1, 2, and 3, can be used simultaneously with the earlier studies in the book for the development of the tongue muscles. As the tongue is somewhat fatigued on a daily basis, the muscles will grow stronger, resulting in a cleaner, well coordinated articulation and a good routine initial release of the tone at all dynamics. The remaining Kayser studies will help develop finger control and speed, first in smaller intervals progressing into larger leaps. There is great value in practicing theses studies at slower speeds, which requires careful control, as well as at faster speeds to achieve nimbleness.

The metronomic indications in the Demnitz, Nocentini, and Baermann have been marked carefully to guide the student in understanding the relationship between tempo, mood, and style. Either too fast or too slow will destroy the mood and style objectives. After becoming sensitive to these objectives, the student will instinctively play the pieces at just the right tempo.

Breathing marks are included so that well paced, deep breathing can be emphasized and related to the musical phrase. Good sound is dependent on proper breathing. Playing too long on one breath not only destroys sound but also generates technical mistakes and breakdowns. An oxygen-starved system does not support an alert mind!

The careful mastery of these studies will certainly make solo repertoire more accessible, and will, in the mean time, provide the saxophonist many joyful hours of musical performance.

DAVID HITE

Please refer to the back cover of this volume for additional study materials to be used in conjunction with and following *Melodious and Progressive Studies, Book 1.*

BIOGRAPHICAL SKETCHES

DEMNITZ, Friedrich, was born in Wunschendorf in 1845, and died in Dresden in 1890 at the age of 45. He received his musical training at the Dresden Conservatory. In 1868 he joined the orchestra at the Court of Mecklenburg-Schwerin, and in 1875 became first clarinetist in the court orchestra of Dresden. He was appointed Professor or Clarinet at the Dresden Conservatory that same year. He became internationally known for his *Clarinetten Schule*, published by both Breitkopf & Hartel and Peters.

NOCENTINI, Dominico, born in 1848, died in Florence, Italy, in 1924. He served as Professore di Clarinetto at the Royal Conservatorio di Musica di Firenze. Among his works for clarinet are the *24 Melodious Studies*, *50 Studi di Meccanismo* for clarinet, *40 Duets*, and a *Fantasia*.

BAERMANN, Carl was born in Munich in 1810 and died there seventy-five years later in 1885. Like his father, the great clarinet virtuoso Heinrich Baermann, for whom Von Weber wrote most of his clarinet compositions (the *Concertino*, the f minor and Eb major *Concertos*, the *Variations, Opus 33*, and the *Clarinet Quintet*), Carl was a prolific composer of clarinet music. Many of his compositions were included in his grand method for clarinet, opus 63. Carl was also a basset horn performer and gave many duo concerts with his father. It was for the Baermanns that Mendelssohn composed the two *Concert Pieces* for clarinet, basset horn and piano.

KAYSER, Heinrich Ernst was born in Altona in 1815 and died in Hamburg in 1888. At the age of 25 he was engaged as a theater violinist in Hamburg where he played until 1857. He then became an independent violin teacher in Hamburg. His violin studies became standard with violin teachers internationally.

HITE, David (1923-2004) studied clarinet with Fred Weaver (Sousa band clarinet), Daniel Bonade and Rosario Mazzeo. He taught woodwinds at Capital University in Columbus, Ohio, from 1954 through 1979. After a career of teaching and playing professionally in Ohio, Mr. Hite became president of David Hite, Inc. a company devoted to the development and production of high quality clarinet and saxophone mouthpieces. Together with his wife Jean, he produced the J&D HITE and PREMIERE lines of mouthpieces which are distributed worldwide. After living for three years in Englewood, New Jersey (near New York City) where he conferred with the world's great clarinetists, he spent his remaining years in Ft. Myers, Florida.

PRACTICE

Think about this: 90% of your playing time in your early development is spent practicing -- practicing by *yourself*. Therefore, those who progress most rapidly are those who become most proficient in well organized self-guidance. The most valuable teacher you have is yourself. You can gather helpful information from a variety of sources (private teachers, school class teachers, band and orchestra directors, classmates, and contest adjudicators) and by listening to great music. This input will help you form a clear idea of how you want to sound. When your objectives are clear, you will know exactly what you want to achieve, and you will improve the efficiency of your practice. Listen carefully to recordings, radio, television, and best of all, live performances. As your listening improves, your ability to guide yourself will improve.

Ideally, you should be practicing an hour or more each day. At a minimum, you should be spending forty five minutes a day practicing. It might be well for you to practice in two shorter periods rather than in one very long sitting. At the end of an overly long practice session your embouchure will tire out and lead you into poor playing habits. Plan to practice six days in a row, then take one day off. The day off is very beneficial (only, however, after you have practiced religiously for six straight days!).

Think about your practice and plan it carefully. Write down your objectives. Think about your tone and how you can improve. Discover how to use the tongue to give each note a precise start. Develop accurate rhythm. Train your fingers to move correctly. Study the style of the music and be expressive when you play. Consider problems one at a time, not all at once. Above all, avoid aimless, thoughtless, "deaf" practice. Deaf practice occurs when you do not listen carefully to what you are playing and you ignore your objectives.

Remember, your teachers can guide you, inspire you, encourage you and find opportunities for you to perform. In the end, however, you will be what you make of yourself. As a great dance instructor one yelled out in rehearsal, "If you don't think about it, it's not going to happen."

Practice. Enjoy it. And reap the benefits from it!

DAVID HITE

18 EXPRESSIVE STUDIES
(based upon scales)

FRIEDRICH DEMNITZ (1845-1890)
Dresden, Germany
Transcribed and edited by DAVID HITE

B-379
B-380

C MAJOR

A MINOR

G MAJOR

E MINOR

D MAJOR

B MINOR

* Learn to emphasize the sixteenth notes as you develop the style of this etude.

A MAJOR

7. Moderato assai ♩=84

mf lively and agressive

F# MINOR

8. Poco lento ♩.=50

p

well sustained and with warm espression

E MAJOR

*Be sure not to lose your sound on the sixteenth notes.
 Taa-YAH Taa-YAH Taa-YAH Taa

B-379
B-380

C# MINOR

10.

A♭ MAJOR

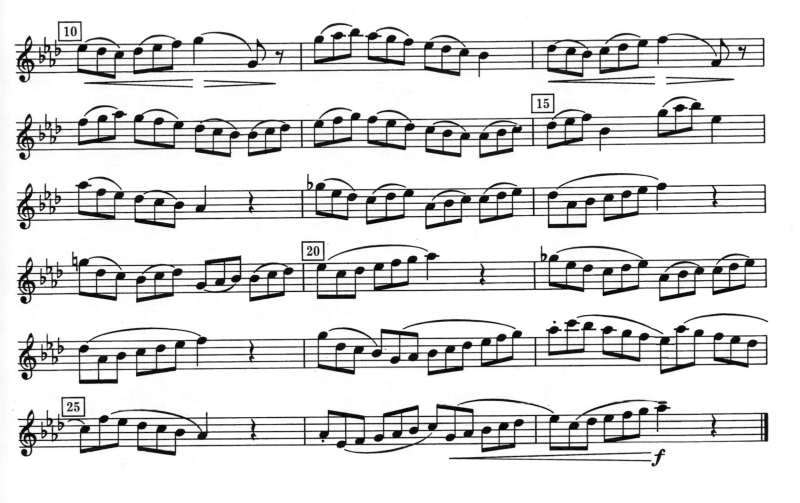

F MINOR

E♭ MAJOR

Allegretto grazioso ♩=116

13.

*The manner in which you emphasize the sixteenth note will style this etude.
Experiment with different degrees to make it gracious and vigorous.

C MINOR

Andante con moto ♩=76

14.

f pleasing, nimble and flowing.

Bb MAJOR

Andante con moto, quasi allegretto ♩.=58

15.

G MINOR

F MAJOR

D MINOR

18.

18 EXPRESSIVE STUDIES
(based upon chords)

F. DEMNITZ (1845-1890)
Transcribed by DAVID HITE

C MAJOR

A MINOR

F MAJOR

D MINOR

B♭ MAJOR

17

G MINOR

E♭ MAJOR

Alla marcia maestoso ♩=104

7.

f bold and firm

C MINOR

8.

Andante con moto ♩.=54

mp

flowing with animation

20

A♭ MAJOR

F MINOR

B-379
B-380

E MAJOR

C# MINOR

A MAJOR

F# MINOR

D MAJOR

B MINOR

G MAJOR

E MINOR

9 MELODIC STUDIES

DOMENICO NOCENTINI, (1848-1924)
Florence, Italy
Transcribed and edited by
DAVID HITE

E MINOR

B MINOR

B-379
B-380

G MINOR

C MAJOR

F MAJOR

G MAJOR

G MAJOR

7. Andantino mosso ♩=84

mf pleasing, moving ahead always

D MINOR

D MINOR

14 MELODIC ETUDES
Opus 63

CARL BAERMANN (1810-1885)
Munich, Germany
Transcribed and Edited by DAVID HITE

C MAJOR

B-379
B-380

C MAJOR

A MINOR

A MINOR

E MINOR

F MAJOR

G MAJOR

46

B-379
B-380

D MINOR

B MINOR

A MAJOR

A MAJOR

B♭ MAJOR

G MINOR

E♭ MAJOR

4 PROGRESSIVE STUDIES
Opus 20

HEINRICH KAYSER (1815-1888)
Hamburg, Germany
Transcribed and Edited by DAVID HITE

This is a very important type of daily exercise that is needed for the development
of the muscles of the tongue. Firm hard strokes of the tongue should be used to
develop strength. Nimble speed will develop, along with coordination, as the
tongue becomes strong. Use rythms:

60

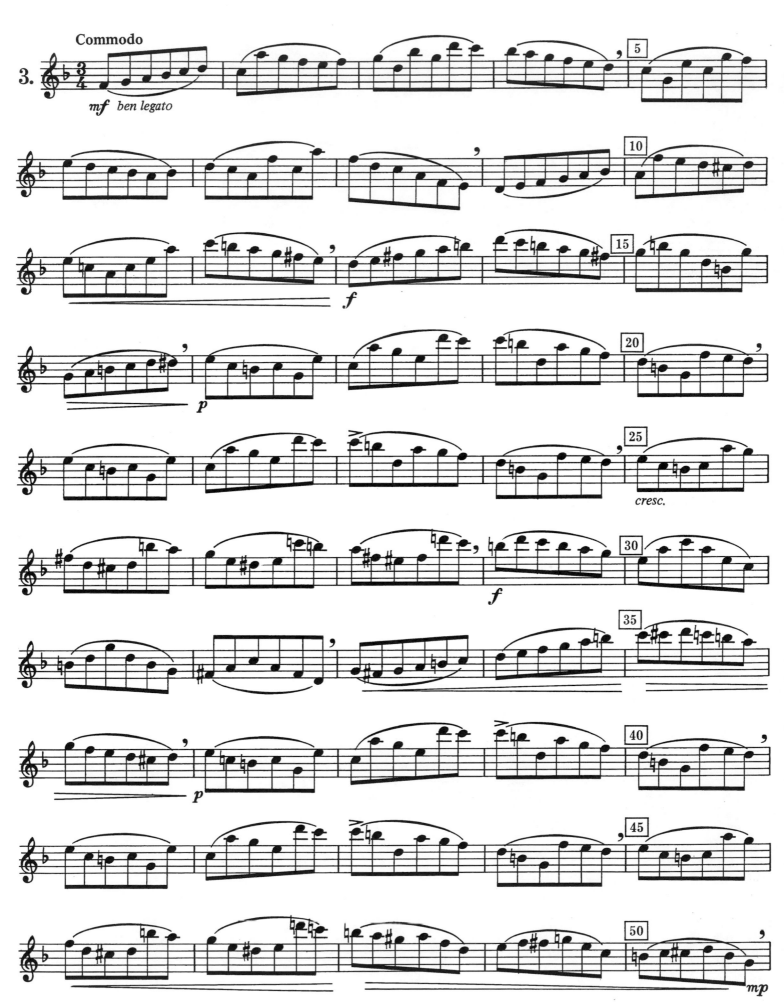

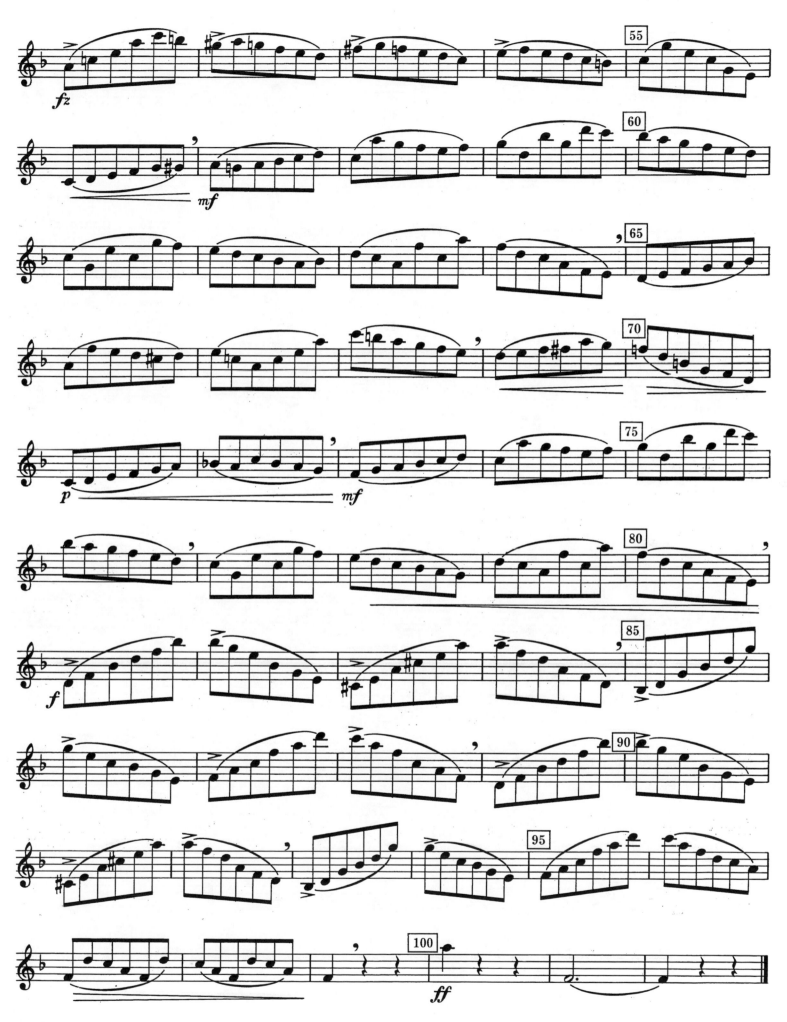

62

MAJOR AND MINOR SCALES

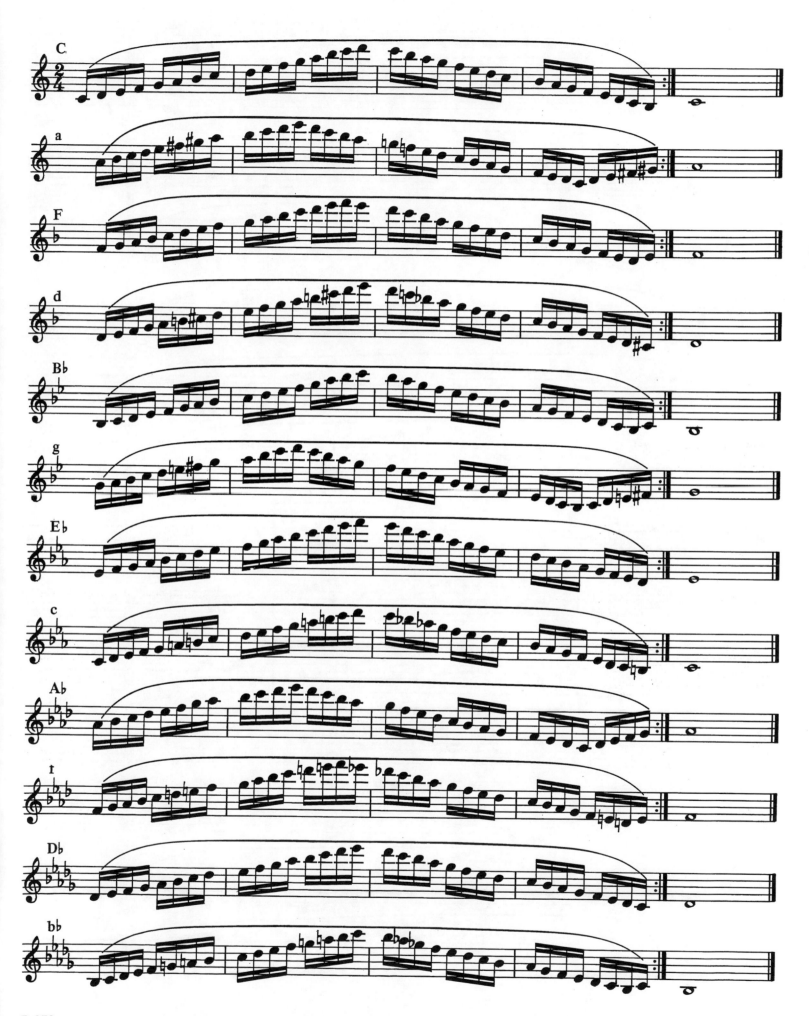

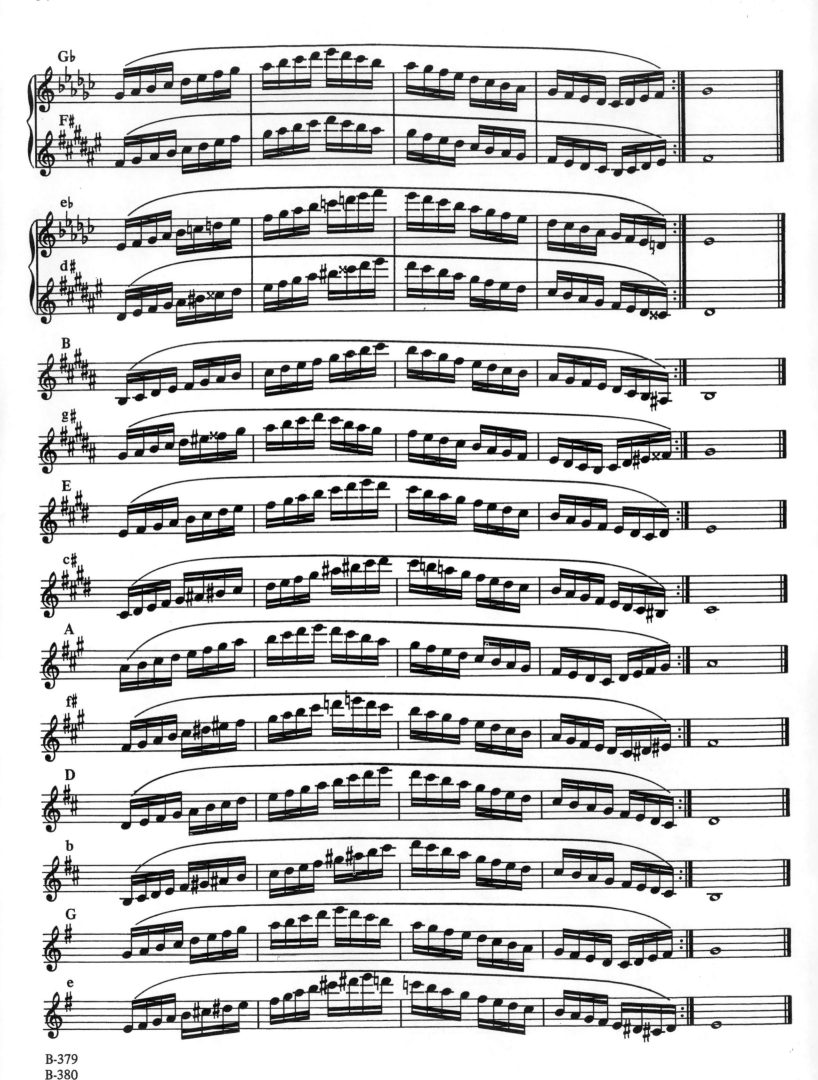